JESUS 101

Jesus
SACRED FRIEND

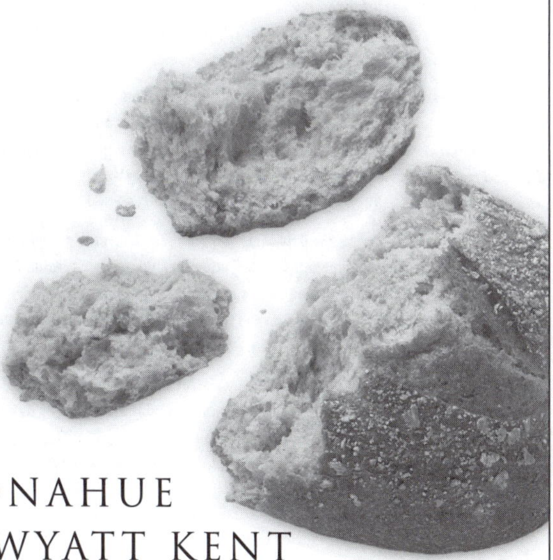

BILL DONAHUE
& KERI WYATT KENT

InterVarsity Press
Downers Grove, Illinois

Inter-Varsity Press
Leicester, England

InterVarsity Press, USA
P.O. Box 1400, Downers Grove, IL 60515-1426, USA
World Wide Web: www.ivpress.com
E-mail: mail@ivpress.com

Inter-Varsity Press, England
38 De Montfort Street, Leicester LE1 7GP, England
Website: www.ivpbooks.com
E-mail: ivp@ivp-editorial.co.uk

©2005 by William Donahue and the Willow Creek Association

All rights reserved. No part of this publication may be reproduced, stored in a retrieval system or transmitted in any form or by any means, electronic, mechanical, photocopying, recording or otherwise, without the prior permission of InterVarsity Press.

InterVarsity Press®, USA, is the book-publishing division of InterVarsity Christian Fellowship/USA®, a student movement active on campus at hundreds of universities, colleges and schools of nursing in the United States of America, and a member movement of the International Fellowship of Evangelical Students. For information about local and regional activities, write Public Relations Dept., InterVarsity Christian Fellowship/USA, 6400 Schroeder Rd., P.O. Box 7895, Madison, WI 53707-7895, or visit the IVCF website at <www.intervarsity.org>.

Inter-Varsity Press, England, is the publishing division of the Universities and Colleges Christian Fellowship (formerly the Inter-Varsity Fellowship), a student movement linking Christian Unions in universities and colleges throughout Great Britain, and a member movement of the International Fellowship of Evangelical Students. For information about local and national activities write to UCCF, 38 De Montfort Street, Leicester LE1 7GP, email us at email@uccf.org.uk, or visit the UCCF website at www.uccf.org.uk.

All Scripture quotations, unless otherwise indicated, are taken from the Holy Bible, New International Version®. NIV®. Copyright © 1973, 1978, 1984 by International Bible Society. Used by permission of Zondervan Publishing House. Distributed in the U.K. by permission of Hodder and Stoughton Ltd. All rights reserved. "NIV" is a registered trademark of International Bible Society. UK trademark number 1448790.

Design: Cindy Kiple
Images: John T. Merkle

USA ISBNs 0-8308-2152-X
           978-0-8308-2152-5

UK ISBNs   1-84474-117-6
           978-1-84474-117-5

Printed in the United States of America ∞

P	19	18	17	16	15	14	13	12	11	10	9	8	7	6	5	4	3	2	1
Y	19	18	17	16	15	14	13	12	11	10	09	08	07	06	05				

CONTENTS

Before You Begin 5

INTRODUCTION: JESUS OUR SACRED FRIEND 11

    1 Jesus Desires Our Friendship 13

    2 Jesus Touches Our Hearts 18

    3 Jesus Guards Our Trust 23

    4 Jesus Shares Our Suffering 29

    5 Jesus Recognizes Our Weaknesses 35

    6 Jesus Celebrates Our Successes 41

Notes for Leaders 47

BEFORE YOU BEGIN

The Jesus 101 series is designed to help you respond to Jesus as you encounter him in the stories and teachings of the Bible, particularly the Gospel accounts of the New Testament. The "101" designation does not mean "simple"; it means "initial." You probably took introductory-level courses in high school or at a university, like Economics 101 or Biology 101. Each was an initial course, a first encounter with the teachings and principles of the subject matter. I had my first encounter with economic theory in Econ 101, but it was not necessarily simple or always easy (at least not for me!).

Jesus 101 may be the first time you looked closely at Jesus. For the first time you will encounter his grace and love, be exposed to his passion and mission, and get a firsthand look at the way he connects with people like you and me. Or perhaps, like me, you have been a Christian many years. In that case you will encounter Jesus for the first time all over again. Often when I read a biblical account of an event in Jesus' life, even if the text is very familiar to me, I am amazed at a new insight or a fresh, personal connection with Jesus I hadn't experienced before.

I believe Jesus 101 will challenge your thinking and stir your soul regardless of how far along the spiritual pathway you might be. After all, Jesus is anything but dull: he tended to shake up the world of everyone who interacted with him. Sometimes people sought him out; often he surprised them. In every case, he challenged them, evoking a reaction they could hardly ignore.

There are many ways we might encounter Jesus. In this series we will focus on eight. You will come face to face with Jesus as

- Provocative Teacher
- Sacred Friend
- Extreme Forgiver
- Authentic Leader
- Truthful Revealer
- Compassionate Healer
- Relentless Lover
- Supreme Conqueror

☐ How These Guides Are Put Together

In each of the discussion guides you will find material for six group meetings, though feel free to use as many meetings as necessary to cover the material. That is up to you. Each group will find its way. The important thing is to encounter and connect with Christ, listen to what he is saying, watch what he is doing—and then personalize that encounter individually and as a group.

The material is designed to help you engage with one another, with the Bible and with the person of Jesus. The experiences below are designed to guide you along when you come together as a group.

Gathering to Listen

This short section orients you to the material by using an illustration, a quote or a text that raises probing questions, makes provocative assumptions or statements, or evokes interpersonal tension or thoughtfulness. It may just make you laugh. It sets the tone for the dialogue you will be having together. Take a moment here to connect with one another and focus your attention on the reading. Listen carefully as thoughts and emotions are stirred.

After the reading, you will have an opportunity to respond in some way. What are your first impressions, your assumptions, disagreements, feelings? What comes to mind as you read this?

Encountering Jesus

Here you meet Jesus as he is described in the Bible text. You will encounter his teachings, his personal style and his encounters with people much like you. This section will invite your observations, questions and initial reactions to what Jesus is saying and doing.

Joining the Conversation

A series of group questions and interactions will encourage your little community to engage with one another about the person and story of Jesus. Here you will remain for a few moments in the company of Jesus and of one another. This section may pose a question about your group or ask you to engage in an exercise or interaction with one another. The goal is to discover a sense of community as you question and discover what God is doing.

Connecting Our Stories

Here you are invited to connect your story (life, issues, questions, challenges) with Jesus' story (his teaching, character and actions). We look at our background and history, the things that encourage or disappoint us. We seek to discover what God is doing in our life and the lives of others, and we develop a sense of belonging and understanding.

Finding Our Way

A final section of comments and questions invites you to investigate next steps for your spiritual journey as a group and personally. It will evoke and prompt further action, decisions or conversations in response to what was discovered and discussed. You will prompt one another to listen to God more deeply, take relational risks and invite God's work in your group and in the community around you.

Praying Together

God's Holy Spirit is eager to teach you! Remember that learning is not just a mental activity; it involves relationship and action. One educator suggests that all learning is the result of failed expectations. We hope, then, that at some point your own expectations will fail, that you will be ambushed by the truth and stumble into new and unfamiliar territory that startles you into new ways of thinking about God and relating to him through Christ. And so prayer—talking and listening to God—is a vital part of the Jesus 101 journey.

If you are seeking to discover Jesus for the first time, your prayer can be a very simple expression of your thoughts and questions to God. It may include emotions like anger, frustration, joy or wonder. If you already have an intimate, conversational relationship with God, your prayer will reflect the deepest longings and desires of your soul. Prayer is an integral part of the spiritual life, and small groups are a great place to explore it.

☐ How Do I Prepare?

No preparation is required! Reading the Bible text ahead of time, if you can, will provide an overview of what lies ahead and will give you an opportunity to reflect on the Bible passages. But you will not feel out of the loop or penalized in some way if you do not get to it. This material is designed for *group* discovery and interaction. A sense of team and community develops and excitement grows as you explore the material together. In contrast to merely discussing what everyone has already discovered prior to the meeting, "discovery in the moment" evokes a sense of shared adventure.

If you want homework, do that after each session. Decide how you might face your week, your job, your relationships and family in light of what you have just discovered about Jesus.

Before You Begin

☐ **A FINAL NOTE**

These studies are based on the book *In the Company of Jesus*. It is not required that you read the book to do any Jesus 101 study—each stands alone. But you might consider reading the parallel sections of the book to enrich your experience between small group meetings. The major sections of the book take up the same eight ways that we encounter Jesus in the Jesus 101 guides. So the eight guides mirror the book in structure and themes, but the material in the book is not identical to that of the guides.

Jesus 101 probes more deeply into the subject matter, whereas *In the Company of Jesus* is designed for devotional and contemplative reading and prayer. It is filled with stories and anecdotes to inspire and motivate you in your relationship with Christ.

I pray and hope that you enjoy this adventure as you draw truth from the Word of God for personal transformation, group growth and living out God's purposes in the world!

INTRODUCTION

OUR SACRED FRIEND

In his book *The Ragamuffin Gospel,* Brennan Manning observes:

> Jesus spent a disproportionate amount of time with people described in the gospels as: the poor, the blind, the lame, the lepers, the hungry, sinners, prostitutes, tax collectors, the persecuted, the downtrodden, the captives, those possessed by unclean spirits, all who labor and are heavy burdened, the rabble who know nothing of the law, the crowds, the little ones, the least, the last, and the lost sheep of the house of Israel.
>
> In short, Jesus hung out with ragamuffins.

In fact, Jesus did more than "hang out" with those on the lower rungs on the social ladder. He seemed to prefer ragamuffins to the religious elite. He extended a hand of friendship across barriers of race, class, ethnicity, color and socioeconomic status.

Though I do not readily identify myself with stuffy, aloof religious leaders, I confess I do not eagerly associate with the "sinners" and "rabble" that Jesus seemed to be drawn to. The last thing I want to be known as is a ragamuffin. Perhaps that's true for you as well. Most of us would prefer the "haves" over the "have-nots." Until we realize we are all have-nots.

It's tempting to pretend that we've got it all together. We may fool even ourselves, believing that accumulations and accomplishments will somehow mend the scars in our soul. We convince ourselves that we can handle things on our own. But in reality—and deep at the core of our soul—we know we need friends. Soul friends. Friends who understand and love us.

When we admit our spiritual poverty and our need for soul friends, we begin to understand our longing to connect with God. As we pay attention to this hunger—a hunger for the company of Jesus—he will move toward us in friendship.

ONE

DESIRES OUR FRIENDSHIP

. . . that you also may be where I am . . .

☐ GATHERING TO LISTEN

Think of a time when someone had a crush on you or someone asked you to join the "inner circle" at work or a teacher gave you extra attention and encouragement or you found a mentor or an acquaintance began to develop into a real friend.

- Describe what happened. How did you feel when that happened? Talk about how the situation affected your self-worth and confidence and any changes or actions it inspired you to make.

Many of us view ourselves as spiritual seekers—looking for truth, insight, wisdom and help from spiritual teachings or people. What we often fail to realize is that God is the supreme seeker, seeking after us. Jesus initiates a relationship with us, because even before we know him, he knows us and desires our fellowship.

- How might the examples above apply to someone's relationship with Jesus?

- Do you think of Jesus as someone who desires your friendship? Why or why not?

☐ ENCOUNTERING JESUS

Whether you are looking for a job, trying to get into the right school or pursuing membership in an exclusive club, the adage usually holds true: "It's not what you know, it's who you know."

We're often flattered when someone above us on the social ladder initiates a friendship, but unfortunately, we're often not very enthused about extending ourselves to those who we consider "beneath" us.

Jesus, on the other hand, seems to be drawn to the "little people" rather than to the movers and shakers. When we begin to realize that he chooses us to be his friends, despite who we really are, the results are life changing.

Read Luke 19:1-9.

Zacchaeus is well known in his town, but no one looks up to him—figuratively or literally. "A short man," he has gained great wealth by collecting taxes from other Israelites, an occupation associated with swindling and extortion. His fellow Jews surely hate him just because of his job.

1. Without using names, do you know anyone like Zacchaeus, someone people despise or reject in your town, on the job or at your school? Why are they viewed this way?

2. Is it possible that you are sometimes like Zacchaeus or a bit like the person you just described? In what way?

3. Jesus says to Zacchaeus, "I *must* stay at your house today." Zacchaeus understands that Jesus is coming to dinner. In Jesus' day, sharing a meal meant much more than it does in our society. It communicated trust, a desire for shared life, friendship and community. In other words, an offer to share a meal was an offer of intimate friendship. Put yourself is Zacchaeus's place. Knowing the cultural implications of sharing a meal, how do you feel knowing that Jesus invites himself to your house for dinner?

☐ JOINING THE CONVERSATION

4. Have you ever noticed an unlikely friendship and wondered, *What does he see in him?* or *What does she see in her?* Look at verse 7. Place yourself in the crowd—how might you feel about Jesus' decision to spend time with Zacchaeus? Why?

5. Recall a time when someone you respect and admire chose to spend time with you. What was it like?

☐ **CONNECTING OUR STORIES**

6. Zacchaeus was never the same again after this dinner with Jesus. Verse 8 describes his change of heart and change of behavior. Has a personal encounter with God changed you in some way, or have you seen a friend or family member change dramatically because of such an encounter? If so, tell the group about it.

7. Read verse 10 again. Consider what you think Jesus means by this statement. In what ways has Zacchaeus been "lost"?

In what ways might you be "lost"?

8. What would your small group community look like a year from now if you followed Jesus' example and extended yourselves relationally to people who, like you and Zacchaeus, need to find their way?

☐ **FINDING OUR WAY**

9. As we work through any story about Jesus, we can apply what we have learned in at least two ways: by reflecting on how we might feel if we were the recipient of Jesus' ministry and by determining to practice Jesus' actions and attitudes.

   What next step might you want to take as a result of reflecting on this encounter? For example, perhaps you want to
   - extend hospitality to someone you normally wouldn't
   - spend more time with Jesus
   - make some change in your behavior or attitudes
   - allow Jesus to "invite himself to dinner at your house"

☐ **PRAYING TOGETHER**

Pray that each group member would have the opportunity to respond to Jesus' offer of friendship and also to extend such friendship to other people.

TWO

Jesus TOUCHES OUR HEARTS

Were not our hearts burning within us?

☐ GATHERING TO LISTEN

Our culture tends to separate the mind from the heart. Ideas and intellectual powers are held in high esteem, while we often neglect the emotions and feelings associated with the heart. The Bible reveals no such dichotomy. The heart, in biblical terms, is more akin to what we today call the mind. It is the governing center of the whole person. It represents the essence of all we are, everything that we think *and* feel. Author John Eldredge explains:

> The heart is central. That we would even need to be reminded of this only shows how far we have fallen from the life we were meant to live—or how powerful the spell has been. The subject of the heart is addressed in the Bible more than any other topic—more than works of service, more than belief or obedience, more than money, and even more than worship. Maybe God knows something we've forgotten. But of course—all those other things are

matters of the heart. . . . The Bible sees the heart as the source of all creativity, courage, and conviction. It is the source of our faith, our hope, and of course, our love. It is the "wellspring of life" within us (Prov. 4:23), the very essence of our existence, the center of our being, the fount of our life. *(Waking the Dead)*

- Do you see your heart the same way Eldredge says the Bible sees it? Why or why not?

☐ ENCOUNTERING JESUS

Jesus touches the heart in each of us—but not with a sloppy sentimentality or irrational emotionalism. When we encounter Jesus, even if we don't recognize him immediately, we are moved profoundly in the deepest part of our being.

Read Luke 24:13-35.

1. Jesus has been crucified, and his followers are bewildered and confused, fearful and uncertain about the future. Sadness prevails over every other emotion. Though they readily talk about what has transpired in Jerusalem (the trial, crucifixion and empty tomb), they remain uncertain of what to make of it. Imagine how these two people may have felt. What is the condition of their hearts?

2. How is it possible that they encounter Jesus and do not "recognize" him?

3. Jesus doesn't immediately reveal his identity to Cleopas and his companion. Why do you think he waits?

4. What have these two people hoped regarding the role Jesus would play in the nation of Israel?

   How may that have kept them from recognizing Jesus (see verse 21)?

☐ **JOINING THE CONVERSATION**
5. Jesus spends several hours with them, explaining truths about himself, yet they do not understand how the events of his death and return to life had been prophesied long before. What causes their spiritual blindness, their inability to see the truth about Jesus?

6. In what ways might we ourselves suffer from spiritual blindness?

7. Jesus says they are "slow of heart" to believe (verses 25-26). Some people have hard hearts, some have open hearts, but what might produce a *slow* heart in someone? In you?

☐ **CONNECTING OUR STORIES**
8. The two exclaim, "Were not our hearts burning within us while he talked?" In other words, God was touching them deeply, stirring their hearts. How would you describe the state of your heart as it relates to God?

9. Have you ever received a touch from God that confirmed his presence in your life and stirred your heart? If so, tell the group about the experience.

☐ Finding Our Way

10. The two on the road realize that they have encountered the living, resurrected Jesus—in person and at the heart level. Are you willing to let God touch your heart?

What do you think might happen as a result?

☐ Praying Together

Ask group members to share an area of their life in which they need Jesus to touch their heart. Pray together that he would touch hearts of individuals and also of the group as a whole.

THREE

GUARDS OUR TRUST

Do not let your hearts be troubled.
Trust in God; trust also in me.

☐ GATHERING TO LISTEN

Many years ago my family invited an ex-convict into our home for a meal to discuss his changed life. My dad and I had attended a banquet for a prison ministry, and the man had given a testimony that was riveting and inspiring. He had met Jesus in prison, and now he was a new man. Members of the audience had been asked to sponsor men like this and help them find their way back into a regular life. The ministry had a program to find them an apartment, help them look for a job and get them back on their feet. They needed some folks like us to serve as friends and mentors.

Soon we had regular interactions with this young man, sharing an occasional meal and providing him an occasional ride when he needed to go to a job interview or to the store. I brought him to church with me. Once he called us late in the evening asking for a ride back to his apartment after a day of work. "Hello, this is Mike. I was supposed to get a ride from my friend Dave, but he had to work later than he thought and can't come get me. I'm stuck out here. Can you help?" We obliged. But then a pattern developed, and a litany of reasons were given for needing rides at odd hours—sick friends, missing buses, people forgetting to pick him up, lost phone numbers.

It did not take long to discover that after work he had been hanging out with his old buddies, using drugs and alcohol, and then needing a ride home. He'd been lying to us and taking advantage of our kindness. We called the ministry, explained the situation and ended our relationship with him. He was removed from the ministry program, having broken trust with us and with the ministry as well.

It was sad. A number of the young men in the program do well at starting a new life. But some wind up like Mike, shunning responsibility and returning to a life of crime.

Sometimes people violate our trust. Corporate scandals, fraud and cheating abound, opening great fractures in the foundation of trust. The result can be that we figure we must put all our faith in our own efforts, wealth and accomplishments. Since we cannot trust others, we'll do life by ourselves. But God wants us to trust him with our life and our future. Can we depend on him for security?

- Psalm 20:7 says, "Some trust in chariots and some in horses, but we trust in the name of the LORD our God." You probably do not have a chariot or a horse. But you trust in other things. What makes you feel secure?

- Are you counting on things like your 401(k) or the status of your job to give you security?

☐ **ENCOUNTERING JESUS**

Jesus often created situations—challenging situations—that provided his disciples the opportunity to exercise trust in him. As you read, think about what you would have done if you were one of the disciples.

Jesus Guards Our Trust 25

Read Matthew 14:22-32.

1. Before digging into this story, make a few observations about Jesus, the Sacred Friend. What do you notice about his spiritual power and his compassion?

2. Imagine yourself as a disciple in the boat. What is your reaction when you see Jesus walking on the water?

3. Does Peter trust Jesus? Explain why or why not in your view.

   What about the rest of the disciples, who stay in the boat? Do they trust Jesus?

☐ **JOINING THE CONVERSATION**

4. Peter's response may seem odd at first. Rather than just leaping out

of the boat, he asks Jesus to tell him to come. Have you ever wished you could say to God, "Just tell me where to go and what to do"?

5. Would you get out of a boat to walk on water if Jesus was telling you to step out? What influences your decision?

6. What happens to Peter when he takes his eyes off Jesus and looks at the wind and waves (see verse 30)?

   How does Jesus guard Peter's trust?

☐ **CONNECTING OUR STORIES**

7. Why is it so hard to trust that God has our best interests in mind?

Did Peter fail? Well, I suppose in a way he did. His faith wasn't strong enough. His doubts were stronger. "He saw the wind." He took his eyes off of where they should have been. He sank. He failed.

But here is what I think. I think there were eleven bigger failures sitting in the boat. They failed quietly. They failed privately. Their failure went unnoticed, unobserved, uncriticized. Only Peter knew the shame of public failure.

But only Peter knew two other things as well. Only Peter knew the glory of walking on water. . . . And only Peter knew the glory of being lifted up by Jesus in a moment of desperate need. . . . He had a shared moment, a shared connection, a shared trust in Jesus that none of the others had.

They couldn't, because they didn't even get out of the boat. The worst failure is not to sink in the waves. The worst failure is to never get out of the boat.

JOHN ORTBERG, *If You Want to Walk on Water, You've Got to Get out of the Boat*

8. After you have read John Ortberg's words in the sidebar, tell of a time you "got out of the boat" but felt as if you failed. Do you think it would have been a bigger failure to avoid taking the risk?

☐ **Finding Our Way**

9. What keeps you in the boat—that is, keeps you from taking risks?

What can you do to "get out of the boat"?

☐ **Praying Together**

Sometimes the first step out of the boat is just to affirm to ourselves and God that we believe he's trustworthy. Consider praying the following verses from Psalm 25 together as a group:

> To you, O Lord, I lift up my soul;
> > in you I trust, O my God. . . .
> Show me your ways, O Lord,
> > teach me your paths;
> guide me in your truth and teach me,
> > for you are God my Savior,
> > and my hope is in you all day long. (verses 1, 4-5)

As you go through your week, take one phrase from this psalm and make it a simple prayer whenever you need to be reminded that Jesus guards our trust. For example, you may want to simply pray, "In you I trust, O my God," several times each day.

FOUR

SHARES OUR SUFFERING

*Because he himself suffered when he was tempted,
he is able to help those who are being tempted.*

☐ GATHERING TO LISTEN

An Olympic runner in the 100-meter dash stumbles and falls at the 50-meter mark. He grabs his leg as searing pain cuts through his muscles like a knife. The attention of the crowd is suddenly focused on the fallen champion. His dreams for victory vanish, and the joy of competing dissolves into anguish. Other runners glance over their shoulder to see what has befallen their foe.

What thoughts run through their minds? Perhaps thoughts like these.

- That's one less person who can rob me of a medal.
- Tough luck, pal.
- Too bad. I'm just glad it wasn't me.
- Serves him right—he pushed it too hard at the start.

Actually, such thoughts never cross the minds of these sprinters. To the wonder of many in the crowd of spectators, the other runners come to a halt and return to help the now-limping athlete. As a group, they encircle the injured competitor, lock arms and begin hobbling along with him, and they cross the finish line as a group. That last 50 meters is filled with laughter, smiles, hugs and words of encouragement. "You can do it! We can do it together!" It is an amazing spectacle.

If you are a fan of the Olympic Games, you may be wondering what year this took place. It was not long ago, but I bet you missed the moment. I did, too. I heard about it later on the news. And yes, it took place in the Olympics—the Special Olympics, where the physically and mentally challenged among us compete against one another. Or, should I say, compete *with* one another. These special athletes got it right, choosing to enter the pain of their friend rather than cross the finish line without him.

The Bible says that when one suffers, we all suffer. It makes all the difference in the world when someone—anyone—chooses to share in our suffering. Jesus is that kind of friend.

- Why is it so difficult for us to willingly enter the suffering of others?
- Tell about a time when you were in pain. How did you feel when people came to be with you in the pain and share your life? Or did you suffer alone?

☐ **ENCOUNTERING JESUS**

Some of us suffer physically, some emotionally, some spiritually. But we all suffer deeply. Pain is disorienting. We experience fear, uncertainty and grief amid our suffering.

Jesus suffered for us—physically, emotionally and spiritually. He was abandoned by friends, mocked by enemies and beaten by the authorities. The Bible teaches that this suffering was necessary to cover our sin and that Jesus took our place when he was on the cross. He suffered with and for us.

Jesus Shares Our Suffering

Read Matthew 26:47-56, 69-75.

1. Jesus is facing the hardest part of his earthly mission—the cross. He knows what is in store for him. How do you suppose he feels, knowing that Judas is going to betray him and Peter will deny him?

Read Matthew 27:27-31.

2. What images or feelings do you have as you encounter Jesus in his suffering?

3. What thoughts come to mind when you ponder the fact that he suffers *willingly*?

☐ **JOINING THE CONVERSATION**

4. Take a moment and reflect on the situations below. In what ways have you suffered at the hands of others?
    - a friend betrayed a confidence
    - you were physically harmed by another person
    - you lost a boyfriend or girlfriend

- an illness caused you great pain
- you experienced a period of despair or depression
- you were treated unfairly at work
- your motives or actions were misrepresented to others
- a close friend or loved one died
- something of great meaning to you was lost or stolen

Describe your feelings during an experience of suffering.

When Chuck Colson, founder of Prison Fellowship, was treated for cancer some years ago, he admitted that we don't know all the reasons that we suffer. But he acknowledged that our suffering and weakness can be an opportunity to witness to the world about the amazing grace of God. Brennan Manning agrees and adds, "Paschal [that is, suffering] spirituality is nothing less than bondage to Jesus Christ alone, a complete attachment to his person, a sharing in the rhythm of his death and resurrection, a participation in his life of sorrow, rejection, loneliness and suffering" (Manning, The Signature of Jesus).

Jesus Shares Our Suffering 33

5. Jesus suffered as you have suffered, and perhaps more so. How does this affect your ability to embrace him as Friend?

☐ **CONNECTING OUR STORIES**

6. Some of us grew up in traditions that, directly or indirectly, made us feel guilty for Christ's sufferings. Discuss as a group how you understood this aspect of Jesus' life in the past. As you discuss this, try to understand and empathize with the spiritual background of other group members.

7. Peter abandons Jesus in the midst of his suffering. Amazingly, Jesus later forgives him for this. But Jesus never abandons us in our suffering. How can your small group serve one another by sharing in each other's suffering?

8. What do you think would happen to the level of community in the group if you entered into each other's sufferings in this way?

☐ Finding Our Way

9. Describe an area in your life where you are experiencing pain, feeling needy or drifting spiritually. What would it look like if Jesus were to come alongside you and share in that confusion and suffering?

☐ Praying Together

Pray for group members who are going through a particularly difficult trial or painful experience. Pray that Jesus would comfort and draw near to those group members, and ask him to reveal to others in the group what they can do to share in that suffering. You may want to close by reading 2 Corinthians 1:3-5 together as a prayer.

FIVE

Jesus RECOGNIZES OUR WEAKNESSES

A time is coming, and has come, when you will be scattered, each to his own home. You will leave me all alone.

☐ GATHERING TO LISTEN

In his book on tennis strategy, *Winning Ugly,* professional tennis coach Brad Gilbert writes that one of the most effective strategies for winning tennis matches is to become a student of your opponent. Notice particularly his weakness. If, for example, your opponent has a weak backhand, keep hitting to his backhand. He'll be much more likely to make a mistake, get frustrated and then make more mistakes, Gilbert explains. Winning means recognizing your opponent's weakness and exploiting it.

Gilbert advises tennis players to "do your own scouting" on opponents. "Look for patterns in their play," he writes. "How do they win points? How do they lose points? . . . Remember what they do at game point or set point. You'll see a pattern of their weaknesses and strengths.

It's part of what you'll use before the match in your preparation and during the match in deciding how to play."

Many of us approach our whole life in much the same way that Gilbert suggests we play tennis—competitively and ruthlessly. We exploit the weaknesses of others in an attempt to feel better about ourselves. We use knowledge of their frailties to "beat them." After all, we want to win, we want to succeed. Sometimes that means defeating anyone who looks like a competitor, whether in the marketplace, at home or even in Christian ministry or service.

- Have you experienced this kind of drive to win? For example, have you ever found yourself trying to "win" in ministry or family matters?

Because weaknesses can be used against us, we hide our own. Someone might exploit them to take advantage of us or make us the brunt of a cruel joke. So we don't want to expose our weaknesses to others. As a result, we become spin doctors, hiding our true self and putting on a façade for the world to see.

Jesus sees right through that. He recognizes our weaknesses, but instead of exploiting them for our demise, he uses them for our growth. Despite our weaknesses, he loves us. And we discover a paradox when the strongest person in the universe, Jesus, meets the weakest people on the planet—us: when we admit our sin, he forgives us instead of crushing us. When we lay down our life for his cause, we gain it back in a powerful, mysterious way. When we are weak, his power is released, making us strong.

- How does it make you feel to know that Jesus recognizes your weakness?

☐ **ENCOUNTERING JESUS**
Read Matthew 26:36-46.

1. What do you notice about Jesus in this passage? Describe his mood and demeanor.

2. Jesus takes his closest followers, Peter, James and John, with him to pray. He desires their support while he prays about the suffering that lies ahead. What does he ask them to pray for, and why?

3. Look at verses 42-44. What is the cup Jesus is referring to, and why is it the focus of his prayer?

☐ **JOINING THE CONVERSATION**

4. As you look again at verse 41, what does Jesus recognize in his disciples?

   How is that very true of us as well?

5. Have you ever felt so overwhelmed and depressed that you just wanted to sleep? Do you think the disciples may have been feeling that way?

What are other possible reasons for their sleepiness?

☐ **CONNECTING OUR STORIES**

6. Here Jesus puts his small group to the test, but they fail. What tests have you encountered as a group?

How tolerant are you of each other's weaknesses?

7. What do you fear when discussing your weaknesses with others? Use the statements that follow to respond to this question, or add one of your own.

- People will no longer accept me.
- I will have to admit I'm not strong.
- I will not be considered for a promotion at work.
- My marriage will become vulnerable.
- I will lose power and authority.
- People will no longer respect me.
- There is another reason:_____.

8. Once we know that Jesus sees our weaknesses, how does that change our relationship with him?

☐ **FINDING OUR WAY**

9. The first step toward sobriety for alcoholics is to "admit that we are powerless" over addiction. The road to recovery begins with acknowledging weaknesses. Jesus sees our weaknesses. Rather than exploiting them, he offers his strength. How might the strength of Jesus help you deal with your weaknesses with authenticity and hope?

☐ **PRAYING TOGETHER**

While Jesus recognizes the weak and broken parts of ourselves, it is sometimes harder for *us* to recognize them. Take a few moments to be quiet. Think about an area of your life where you are weak. Sit in quiet reflection, allowing each group member to pray silently about their particular struggle.

End this time by praying out loud together: "Your grace is sufficient for me, for your power is made perfect in weakness. Lord, you know our weaknesses. Meet them with your power and grace. Set us free from the things that overpower us."

SIX

Jesus Celebrates Our Successes

Anyone who has faith in me will do what I have been doing.
He will do even greater things than these.

☐ Gathering to Listen

When I finished my doctoral studies, the time for graduation arrived. I had started the program while living in Texas but then moved to Chicago to take a position at Willow Creek, so I finished the degree and research paper while living in Illinois. I told Gail that I was probably not going to fly back to Texas and attend the graduation exercises. Yes, I had worked hard over a six-year period, but I did not need to go to another graduation ceremony. They all start to look alike after a while. And the money we would have spent on plane tickets and a graduation gown could be saved for something more worthwhile.

"Look, buddy," my wife said, "we all sacrificed so that you could earn that Ph.D. This has been a long, hard road for everyone, and we are going to celebrate this accomplishment! We are going to Texas, we are attending the ceremony, and afterward we are having a party!"

Needless to say, her opinion prevailed. We flew to Texas, attended the ceremony, and celebrated that afternoon with our family and many friends from the Dallas–Fort Worth area. It was a blast.

What had I been thinking? I almost missed one of the most enjoyable days of my life. The party was *for* me, but it was not all *about* me. It was about friends, family, God and hard work. And I have to admit, it was a real honor and joy to be celebrated by others.

Appreciation and celebration tend to remind us of past victories and motivate us to persevere toward future goals and challenges.

- Have you ever had someone genuinely appreciate and celebrate your success? How did that feel?

☐ Encountering Jesus
Read Luke 10:1-24.

1. Jesus sends his disciples out to preach and teach and heal—to do the things he had been doing. This seems like a risky venture. What might his motivation be for delegating such important responsibilities to his followers?

2. As you read through this passage, what do you discover about the nature of the work Jesus is delegating to the disciples? Why is it so important?

Jesus Celebrates Our Successes 43

3. Put yourself in the disciples' sandals and read verse 3 again. How do you feel as Jesus describes your mission? Compare that with verse 17.

☐ **JOINING THE CONVERSATION**

4. What is the first step toward success for the seventy-two disciples?

   Why do you think Jesus sends them "two by two"?

5. Have you ever been sent out to accomplish a mission? If so, how did the instruction and support of the person sending you affect the outcome of your mission?

6. In verse 20, Jesus gets to the heart of the matter: success is great, but what really matters is that you are Jesus' friend, "that your names are written in heaven." What do you think he means by that?

What does his statement tell you about Jesus' values?

☐ **CONNECTING OUR STORIES**

Celebration brings joy into life, and joy makes us strong. Scripture tells us that the joy of the Lord is our strength (Neh. 8:10). We cannot continue long in anything without it. Women endure childbirth because the joy of motherhood lies on the other side. Young married couples struggle through the first difficult years of adjustment because they value the insurance of a long life together. Parents hold steady through the teen years, knowing that their children will emerge at the other end human once again.

Celebration is central to all the Spiritual Disciplines. Without a joyful spirit of festivity the Disciplines become dull, death-breathing tools in the hands of modern Pharisees.

RICHARD FOSTER, *Celebration of Discipline*

7. Sometimes when we are trying to follow Jesus and serve him, we succeed. But sometimes we don't, or it seems as if we've fallen short. What do you think Jesus would say to us when we feel as if we've failed?

8. Look at verse 21. How does Jesus feel about his disciples' success?

   What does the verse tell us about Jesus and our place in his kingdom?

☐ **FINDING OUR WAY**

9. What might your mission as a small group be?

10. If you have the opportunity to lead others—in ministry, in the workplace, in your family—what might result if you begin to rejoice in their successes?

☐ **PRAYING TOGETHER**

Spend some time thanking God for celebrating your life. Jesus wants you to know that you matter and that your life is worth living. He longs to support you and encourage you as you seek him and obey his truth. Have you given Jesus credit for your successes, or do you think they are due entirely to your effort and abilities?

Ask Jesus to help you succeed in what he's called you to do. Ask him also for the proper perspective on the reasons for your success. Thank him that he loves you the same whether you seem to be successful or not.

NOTES FOR LEADERS

Each session has a similar format using the components below. Here is a very rough guide for the amount of time you might spend on each segment for a ninety-minute meeting time, excluding additional social time. This is a general guide, and you will learn to adjust the format as you become comfortable working together as a group:

Gathering to Listen	5-10 minutes
Encountering Jesus	15 minutes
Joining the Conversation	20 minutes
Connecting Our Stories	20 minutes
Finding Our Way	10 minutes
Praying Together	about 10 minutes

You can take some shortcuts or take longer as the group decides, but strive to stay on schedule for a ninety-minute meeting including prayer time. You will also want to save time to attend to personal needs and prayer. This will vary by group and can also be accomplished in personal relationships you develop between meetings.

As group leader, know that you help create an environment for spiritual growth. Here are a few things to consider as you invite people to follow in the company of Jesus.

Leader Tips

Practice authenticity and truth telling. Do not pretend an elephant is not sitting in the middle of the room when everyone knows it is.

- Does your group have a commitment to pursue personal change and growth?
- Set some ground rules or a covenant for group interactions. Consider values like confidentiality, respect and integrity.
- Model and encourage healthy self-disclosure through icebreakers, storytelling and getting to know one another between meetings.

Connecting Seekers to Jesus

This simple process is designed to help you guide a person toward commitment to Christ. It is only a guide, intended to give you the feel of a conversation you might have.

1. Describe what you see going on. "Mike, I sense you are open to knowing Jesus more personally. Is this the case?"

2. Affirm that Jesus is always inviting people to follow him (John 6:35-40). "Mike, Jesus has opened the door to a full and dynamic relationship with him. All who believe in Jesus are welcome. Do you want to place your trust in Jesus?"

3. Describe how sin has separated us from God, making a relationship with God impossible (Romans 3:21-26). "Though Jesus desires fellowship with us, our sin stands in the way. So Jesus went to the cross to pay for that sin, to take away the guilt of that sin and to make reconciliation with God possible again. Are you aware that your sin has become a barrier between you and Jesus?"

4. Show how Jesus' death on the cross bridged the gap between us and God (Romans 5:1-11). "Now we can have peace with God, a relationship with Jesus, because his death canceled out our sin debt. All our offenses against God are taken away by Jesus."

5. Invite them to have a brief conversation with God (2 Corinthians 5:11—6:2). "By asking for his forgiveness and being reconnected to Jesus, we can have new life, one that starts now. Jesus invites you to join him in this new life—to love him, learn his ways, connect to his people and trust in his purposes. We can talk to him now and express that desire if you want to."

These five suggestions are designed to create a dialogue and discern if a person wants to follow Jesus. Points to remember:

1. Keep dialogue authentic and conversational.
2. God is at work here—you are simply a guide, leading someone toward a step of faith in Jesus.
3. The heart is more important than the specific words.
4. People will not understand all that Christ has done, so don't try to confuse them with too much information.
5. Keep it simple.
6. Don't put words in someone's mouth. Let them describe how they want to follow Jesus and participate in his life.

Notes for Leaders   49

7. Use Scripture as needed. You may recite some or let them read the passages.
8. Remember, this is not a decision to join an organization. It is a relationship with a person, an invitation to a new life and a new community: "Come follow me."

As the person expresses the desire to follow Jesus, encourage them to read the Gospel of Mark and discover the life of Jesus and his teachings more clearly.

SESSION 1.
JESUS DESIRES OUR FRIENDSHIP.
Luke 19:1-9

Gathering to Listen (2-3 minutes). Everyone does not need to answer; those who do should pick one item on the list and give a brief example. You may want to say, "I'm sure we've all experienced at least one of these. Let's hear one or two experiences of each of the items on this list." Try to lead the conversation away from long stories, but get to the heart of what made the relationship meaningful.

Remind group members that Jesus is the initiator in our spiritual life. Even if we are "seeking," he seeks us as well. Get the group to discuss the parallels between their human relationships and their friendship with Jesus, and also how they differ.

Encountering Jesus (15 minutes). Religious leaders in Jesus' day were known for "pulling rank" socially. They would never associate with someone like Zacchaeus—tax collectors were typically Jews who had gone to work for the oppressive Roman government. They were considered traitors; it would be almost like a Jew's working for the Nazi government during World War II.

Jesus was, of course, not like other religious leaders of his day. But did Zacchaeus know that? He was trying to get a better look, to see what Jesus was like. He knew this teacher-rabbi was different, but he didn't know just how different. He might have expected Jesus to despise him, or ignore him, or even rebuke him.

To get an idea of the typical attitude of religious leaders toward tax collectors, read Luke 18:9-14.

Encourage the group to imagine themselves in the story, to put themselves in the place of the various characters. Help members consider how Zacchaeus responds to Jesus' initiative. How would they feel if they were Zacchaeus? What do they imagine is going through his mind as he interacts with Jesus?

Joining the Conversation (20 minutes). These questions are designed to get into people's views and perspectives. Be aware here of how people view themselves. It may be hidden in their comments about why they are surprised that Jesus spent time with Zacchaeus or why Zacchaeus is not worthy to be with Jesus. Perhaps they feel unworthy to be close to Jesus. Many people believe they have done something that separates them so far from God that the gap cannot be closed. Help them begin to grasp the lavish grace and love of God.

Connecting Our Stories (20 minutes). We often emphasize our own spiritual seeking, but what does it mean that Jesus "came to seek"? Help participants understand that they are the object of Jesus' desire—that he moves toward us as Sacred Friend.

As you are discussing these questions, you can take people a step deeper by simply listening to their responses, then following up with a question like "How do you feel about that?" Someone may admit they never thought that Jesus might desire fellowship with them. Ask them how that makes them feel. Why did they assume Jesus' disinterest in them?

In Luke 19:9-10 Jesus refers to Zacchaeus as one who is lost. The questions here are designed to help people look honestly at their relationship with God. This may lead to a level of vulnerability that is new in your group. Here are some insights that may help you sort out the issues with them.

Some are "lost" because they are far from the God who loves them and reaches out to them in Christ. God is building a new community, a new family, and is seeking sons and daughters to join it. Some in your group may be wandering aimlessly, drifting far from sources of truth and wisdom. Christ-followers can experience a kind of "lostness" as well. Though their eternity is secure in Christ, they are drifting. It may be because of sin or despair. God has not left them, but they feel a distance, a disconnect from God.

A final note. In this passage Zacchaeus is called a son of Abraham, and Jesus says that salvation has come to his house. Jesus had already asserted that he came first to the house of Israel (Matthew 15:24; John 4:22), and the apostle Paul says that salvation came to the Jews first (Romans 1:16). In other words, despite what Zacchaeus's reputation may have been, since he was a Jew, the offer of salvation in Christ was in effect for him. Jews were the first to see the Messiah Jesus—but not the only ones. Though the gospel was first offered to Jews, it was for Gentiles too. Jesus was simply saying that Zacchaeus was just as deserving of the offer of salvation as any other Jew. And every one of us, Jew or Gentile, is a son or daughter of Abraham, our spiritual father, who chose to follow God by faith and pointed the way to Jesus (Genesis 12:1-3; 15:1-6).

Finding Our Way (10 minutes). Encourage group members to practice what they have learned. Watch, however, for overenthusiastic group members who get the "new year's resolution" mentality, promising to radically alter behavior or attitudes. Stress that each person should pray and ask God what a next step of faith might be in an area they are trying to change. Don't let participants stop at just selecting one of these answers, but probe how—specifically—they plan to carry out their actions.

Praying Together (about 10 minutes). Again, emphasize small steps. Ask, "What one small step do you think God might be prompting you to take?"

SESSION 2.
JESUS TOUCHES OUR HEARTS.
Luke 24:13-35

Gathering to Listen (8-10 minutes). Be clear on what the Bible is talking about with respect to the heart—the truest, realest part of us—compared to what our culture means by the word. You may want to get the group to brainstorm what they think when they hear the word *heart*. They may think of courage (as in "he's got a lot of heart") or emotions and sentimentality, the opposite of what's in our "head." Affirm that our culture sees it this way, but contrast these with how the Bible sees the heart—and it is our heart as the Bible describes it that Jesus wants to touch. See B. O. Banwell, "Heart," in *New Bible Dictionary*, 3rd ed., ed. I. Howard Marshall, A. R. Millard, J. I. Packer and D. J. Wiseman (Downers Grove, Ill.: InterVarsity Press, 1996), p. 456.

Encountering Jesus (15 minutes). Encourage participants to look for clues in the story that reveal the feelings of these two people. These two followers had been in Jerusalem for the Passover and had likely seen all the events leading to Jesus' crucifixion. Apparently God has supernaturally kept these two from recognizing Jesus, though we do not know exactly why. Perhaps Jesus wants to wait and reveal himself at the right time. (Some scholars believe Cleopas was Jesus' uncle, brother of Joseph and father of Simeon. If so, certainly he would have recognized Jesus had not there been divine intervention to mask his identity.)

The two are sullen (verse 17) concerning the dramatic events of the past few days. They are also a bit confused because of the empty tomb. Jesus takes them through many Scriptures of the Old Testament—from Moses and the Prophets—to show that this Jesus was the Messiah, the One whose coming to rescue Israel had been foretold. The rebuke "How foolish you are!" (verse 25) points to the fact that though as good Jews they had heard the Scriptures read every week in the local synagogue, they had not linked these prophecies with the events that have recently taken place.

Instead, they have been confused; they say they had hoped "that he was the one who was going to redeem Israel." Certainly they are heartbroken that Jesus has proved not to be the Messiah—or why would he have been killed by the Romans, the very people the Jews expected the Messiah to overcome?

The breaking of the bread is the moment of truth. There is more here than simply the sharing of a meal. Jesus waits to be officially invited in—typical hospitality in that day toward strangers one might meet on the road. One cannot help but think of Revelation 3:20, where Jesus knocks at the door and awaits our invitation to come in. Table scenes in a home appear frequently in Luke's writing (see Luke 5:29; 7:36; 10:38-40; 14:1, 7, 12, 15-16). In this culture it was the place to express friendship and hospitality. Much of Jesus' ministry took place at meals in people's homes.

Whether it is the way Jesus breaks the bread or God's opening their eyes—or likely both—immediately the disciples recognize Jesus. Perhaps they see the scars on his hands. Perhaps it is the way he prays. Or perhaps they had heard the story of the Last Supper from Jesus' closest disciples and recognize the manner in which he breaks the bread and speaks to them. In any case, God has opened their eyes, and immediately Jesus "disappeared"—evidence that he is in his resurrected body and no longer bounded by all the limitations of space and time.

Joining the Conversation (20 minutes). Try to get at what causes spiritual blindness, both in the story and in the lives of group members. It is easiest to start by looking at the people in the story, who were blinded by their grief and disappointment. Then ask, "Have you ever felt like the people in this story?" We are easily blinded by our own agendas and expectations. The Jews wanted a political or military Messiah, and Jesus did not fit the description. Unbelievers are blinded by the evil one (see 2 Corinthians 4:4).

So sin, ignorance or the evil one may be the cause of spiritual blindness. Any of these reasons may cause a heart to be slow at recognizing and receiving truth about God.

Connecting Our Stories (20 minutes). When we encounter spiritual truth, often our "hearts burn within us": we are spiritually awakened to the work of God. But sometimes we don't recognize the intense emotion as marking an encounter with Jesus. Allow group members to recount any experience in which their heart was touched, even if it doesn't seem "spiritual." Help members reflect on where God might have been present in that situation, perhaps in a way they were not aware of in that moment.

A touch from God may come at the funeral of a friend, a celebration of someone's marriage or the simple caress of a baby's face. As we interact with God and his creation, we encounter his presence. In some cases, Jesus makes that presence very deep and personal. "Where two or three come together in my name, there am I with them" (Matthew 18:20).

For those who do not know Jesus personally, encourage them to consider that God may be at work in them, that Jesus may be moving toward them as a sacred friend. In moments when they feel prompted toward spiritual discovery and insight, it may be that Jesus is seeking them, extending his hand in friendship.

Finding Our Way (10 minutes). In order to allow Jesus to move in our heart, we have to make our heart receptive to him. If group members are not ready, ask them to just think about the possibility of letting Jesus touch their heart right now. Perhaps a time of silence and reflection will help.

Praying Together (about 10 minutes). After asking group members to risk expressing their feelings and exposing their hearts, move into a time of prayer. Make your prayer time a safe time for group members: avoid using prayer to preach or attempt to change anyone in the group. You may want to break into groups of two or three so that participants can discuss in a more personal way how God is working in them. But use your judgment as to whether smaller groupings will help or hinder sharing.

SESSION 3.
JESUS GUARDS OUR TRUST.
Matthew 14:22-32

Gathering to Listen (7-8 minutes). The verse from Psalms has an old-fashioned sound, far from our time and place. Try to get the group to paraphrase it. For example, some trust in power, some trust in money, some trust in a new SUV or an expensive home—all the modern-day equivalents of a horse or a chariot. Others may put trust in a career or even in their religious activities.

Focus on what it means to trust in God. Members may be at different levels on this. Spiritual seekers may not be sure God is worth their trust. Religious hypocrisy, a bad church experience or their own fears may stand in the way. To place trust in someone requires action: you do not just talk about trusting but actually act in a way that demonstrates it.

Encountering Jesus (15 minutes). This story, repeated in Mark 6 and John 6, is one of the most popular among Bible readers. It is powerful yet draws us into great introspection, a test of faith for everyone who encounters Jesus. Jesus has just finished feeding the five thousand, and the people want to make him king (another indication that they saw him as a conquering, not suffering, Messiah). He sends the disciples on their way ahead of him because he needs to deal with the crowd. The suggestion is, this will take some time. Jesus doesn't want to be crowned king, and the frenzied crowd needs to be calmed down and sent home. Afterward he spends several hours in prayer.

It is speculated that the prayer is prompted by the desire to make him king. Like the temptation from Satan in Matthew 4 (where Jesus was offered all the kingdoms of the world to rule), this may have tempted Jesus. He needs to be with his Father alone, perhaps to receive instruction or wisdom or to remain focused on his mission. Jesus draws strength from the Father in prayer, and he has just expended great energy teaching and doing miracles.

The boat has traveled only two to three miles from shore westward into the storm and against a strong headwind while Jesus is with the crowd and in prayer. So there is no possibility that Jesus is walking at the shallow edges of the lake. Normally, a few hours might have been enough for the disciples' boat to cross the entire lake (about seven miles at the widest part), but a strong wind and rough seas have made the trip pure drudgery. Presumably they are headed first to Bethsaida, where Jesus will catch up with them, and then to Capernaum. But Jesus has been gone a considerable time and the storm is rough. So Jesus walks to meet them in the fourth watch of the night, between 3:00 and 6:00 a.m.

Naturally, the disciples are afraid—terrified, the text tells us. So the first thing Jesus tells his friends is the single most oft-repeated command in the Bible: "Don't be afraid." We are often fearful people, and God knows us well. The fact that he so often tells us "Fear not" indicates his love for is and his desire to have us trust him.

Peter may have been one of the oldest among the Twelve. His impetuous response reflects his desire to follow Jesus and to be an example—a leader—to the others. Peter trusts Jesus enough to listen to him and to act accordingly. His actions may seem strange to us, but disciples of rabbis in Jesus' day followed their teacher everywhere, doing and saying what they were told. So it makes sense that Peter would want to do what Jesus is doing.

Joining the Conversation (20 minutes). It is human nature to look for direction from God. We ask him to guide us, ask him for a sign. But what is it that we are really asking? And if we receive direction, are we willing to do what God says even if it seems difficult or absurd? Help the group see that God directs us in a variety of ways: through the Bible, through leadings from his Spirit, through the wisdom of others and through wisdom he supplies to us in prayer. But however he leads, he asks us to trust him. Focus on Peter's trust level and his ability to obey.

Connecting Our Stories (20 minutes). Obedience doesn't guarantee success. But Peter did best when he kept his eyes on Jesus rather than the waves. Discuss what it means to keep our eyes on Jesus in the midst of difficult circumstances. Peter is literally on the water, looking at the physical person of Jesus. Jesus literally reaches out and grabs Peter. In our day, looking at Jesus and taking his hand are not things we can do in a physical and literal sense. So the story applies differently to us. We can embrace Jesus because, as Christ-followers, we have the risen Jesus dwelling in us. We can "walk on water" like Peter if we trust in the power of Jesus to help us meet the difficulties of life by faith. This is where you want the group to go. Don't stop at "I should keep my eyes on Jesus." Ask members to describe what that means in practical terms.

Note: You may want to read more of John Ortberg's book to prepare for this discussion. He makes a number of astute observations about this passage and how to apply it to our lives.

Finding Our Way (10 minutes). We don't move from total fear to complete trust overnight. Jesus guards our trust so that it is protected and able to grow. He never misuses it, misplaces it or ignores it. Yet we must learn to trust slowly over time by taking steps of faith, even in the midst of doubt. Emphasize the process rather than the result. Ask group members, "What might your next step be in trusting Jesus?"

Even though the disciples proclaim that Jesus is the Son of God, they will later desert him, disobey him and misunderstand him. Like us, they believe in part and know in part. One day we are filled with faith and trust and would do anything for Jesus. The next day we ignore his simplest command or ask, *Does he really care about me?* when we are isolated at home with the flu. We can be fickle. Faith is a journey in which we move forward three steps and then slip back a step or two.

Praying Together (about 10 minutes). A single-sentence prayer is sometimes called a "breath prayer," so named because it can be uttered in a single breath. This type of prayer, repeated quietly throughout the day, has been used for centuries by Christians to focus their attention on God. Encourage participants to combine prayer and meditation on Scripture in this way. You may want to suggest other meaningful verses they can use to guide their prayers.

SESSION 4.
Jesus Shares Our Suffering.
Matthew 26:47-56, 69-75; 27:27-31

Gathering to Listen (5-7 minutes). Connecting with the suffering of others is often a difficult thing to do. We are afraid—afraid that we will not understand, or cannot provide the help they need, or will look foolish. In reality, people usually just want company. They do not want to be alone in their pain.

Look for signs of pain and loneliness in your group as members begin to open up about their own suffering. Have they learned from past sufferings? If so, what? Are they presently carrying a heavy burden of emotional or relational pain? As people share, remember these stories later in the lesson when you "connect" with each other's stories more personally.

Encountering Jesus (15 minutes). *Questions 2-3:* First, focus on the suffering Jesus. Summarize what he endured, though there's probably no need to go into the horrible details of crucifixion and scourging. Look at the range of his suffering. In this short passage we see Jesus mocked, exposed, ridiculed, inflicted with pain, struck, spat upon and led to crucifixion. It is hard to image a worse situation. Earlier we read that he has been betrayed, denied and abandoned. And we know the Father has turned his back. His suffering is at every possible level, and it is intense.

His suffering not only satisfied the judgment of God and made possible our reconciliation with God, but it also made Jesus like us. Hebrews 4:15 and 2:18 are key passages about this. They refer to his temptation at the hands of Satan (Matthew 4:1-17) and his suffering on the cross.

That Jesus suffered willingly is a powerful reality, especially since, as God's Son, he had the powers of the universe at his disposal. Instead he chose to obey his Father, fulfill his mission and redeem us in order to have fellowship with us. "For the joy set before him [he] endured the cross" (Hebrews 12:2).

In regard to *question 3:* Jesus is betrayed (by Judas), and his closest supporter (Peter) denies ever knowing him. The rest of the disciples flee, so Jesus is abandoned.

Abandonment is a terrible thing. Children feel it when parents divorce, spouses feel it when their lifelong partner dies, and we all feel it when friends turn their back on us. Jesus felt this when he quoted Psalm 22 from the cross: "My God, my God, why have you forsaken me?"

Jesus had known the intimacy of Matthew 3:17 and 11:27—connection with the Father that was deeply personal and life giving. Now the Father has turned his back on the Son (see Isaiah 53:6-10). Jesus is alone. He knows what it is like to suffer alone.

Joining the Conversation (20 minutes). What you want the group to get at is that Jesus has experienced many of the same things we have. All of us have had friends who let us down when we needed them most. Remind the group that even though Jesus was divine, he was also human, and part of his humanity was expressed in his desire to be with people, to be in a mutually loving relationship.

He wanted to be in community with his disciples, and so he felt real pain when they let him down, just as we do. He still desires to be in loving, mutual relationship with us. Help the group get in touch with the fact that Jesus has experienced the same pain and disappointment that they have.

Connecting Our Stories (20 minutes). Help participants see that Jesus helps us by bringing other people our way who can share our suffering and provide practical help. He has suffered, and he shares our suffering through others. God meets the needs of people through people. So when we ask Jesus to come alongside and share our suffering, he often answers that request by sending caring people our way.

Challenge the group to be Christ to one another and to others in very practical ways.

Finding Our Way (10 minutes). This part of the session returns to personal reflection. After talking about how the group can function better to walk with each other in pain, here our focus is on seeing Jesus as the Sacred Friend who suffers with us. He extends the hand of friendship toward us, but it is a scarred hand. We do not shrink back from holding it but gratefully embrace it. Those scars mean that he knows our plight and shares our pain.

Pay attention to what God is doing in group members' lives, and remember these concerns as you move into a time of prayer.

Praying Together (about 10 minutes). Again, God's plan to heal and help the suffering of his people is to have us do something to show love and mercy. Challenge group members to either give or accept the gift of Christ's love. That gift can be shared in prayer.

SESSION 5.
Jesus Recognizes Our Weaknesses.
Matthew 26:36-46

Gathering to Listen (7-8 minutes). Encourage the group to be honest about areas where they are competitive—in sports or on the job, for example. Because of our culture's emphasis on winning, it can be very hard to admit a weakness.

Notes for Leaders

But we can't appreciate Jesus' recognition of our weakness unless we are willing to recognize it ourselves.

Being authentic as a leader and making the group a safe place are important when discussing a topic like this. Model acceptance of all group members, and share your own struggles authentically. If people are shamed by others when they confess a weakness, or if you aren't willing to share your story honestly with the group, the conversation will either remain shallow or shut down entirely.

Encountering Jesus (15-20 minutes). Consider how Jesus may feel (betrayed, misunderstood, rejected). His soul is filled with anguish, mirroring the emotions expressed in Psalms 42—43. The prospect of crucifixion—a tortuous and painful death—combined with carrying the sin of the world must be agonizing. After he has wrestled with this in prayer, how do you think he feels when he finds his disciples asleep?

Jesus asks Peter, James and John to stay close and to pray "so that you will not fall into temptation" (see verse 41). This temptation is not likely the temptation to sleep, but rather what Jesus referred to in Matthew 26:31, that they might fall away during trials and then drift away from their developing faith. "Spiritual eagerness is often accompanied by carnal weakness," says D. A. Carson, commenting on this passage (*Matthew*, Expositors Bible Commentary). Jesus wants them to remain close to him but to pray for their own strength. But they are not strong—for him or for themselves.

The "cup" or "hour" in John's description of this event is the suffering endured on the cross, the redemptive work of Christ for our sin. He is in the Garden of Gethsemane, surrounded by olive trees. The word Gethsemane comes from means "oil press." Certainly for Jesus this is strongly symbolic. Earlier this evening he has called himself the "true vine" (John 15), and within a few hours he will be crushed for our sin.

Joining the Conversation (20 minutes). If you have access to a DVD or tape of *The Passion of the Christ*, you may want to have the group watch the first few minutes of this movie, which depict the scene described in Matthew 26:36-46.

"The flesh is willing but the spirit is weak" does not refer to the Holy Spirit but to the weakness of our will. Despite our noble desires to do good, inside we are weak and often unable to rise to the level of our pious aspirations. This is true of each of us—remember the struggle Paul details in Romans 7:14-25.

The disciples may be tired for several reasons. It is late in the evening. Though these three are fisherman and should be accustomed to working late nights and early mornings (see Luke 5:4-5 and John 21:3), they may be exhausted. Perhaps it is the emotional strain of the last few days, the Passover feast and the travel they have completed. Or like most of us, perhaps they are just weak. Ever fall asleep while praying? Imagine trying to pray for an hour, reclining on the ground late in the evening. They allow physical weakness to overcome spiritual desire.

Connecting Our Stories (20 minutes). The focus here is how we can respond to each other's shortcomings in a Christlike way. If a group member or family member admits a weakness, how do you respond? As we encounter the weak and broken parts of one another, we realize how essential it is that we model the life of Christ, who loves us despite our weaknesses.

Nonetheless, opening up is fearful. As members respond to question 9, help them talk freely about the reasons we all hide weaknesses and highlight strengths.

You might want to tell a story about how God used a weakness of yours to demonstrate his strength and power. Knowing that Jesus sees and accepts our weaknesses should give us hope and allow us to relate to him more openly. We have nothing to hide. And he knows what it means to be vulnerable and weak.

Finding Our Way (10 minutes). Like an alcoholic, we may be addicted to work, the approval of others, shopping or any number of other things. Anything that becomes more important than God, or numbs us to the truth or hides our real feelings, can be an addiction. The key is confession of sin and weakness instead of living in denial. Allow members some personal space to do this.

Praying Together (about 10 minutes). Use this prayer to help members admit they need God's help. Saying it together will help participants experience a sense of community and feel a measure of healing and hope.

SESSION 6.
JESUS CELEBRATES OUR SUCCESSES.
Luke 10:1-24

Gathering to Listen (8 minutes). There may be some people in the group who do not have much to celebrate. They may be overcome with failure. Per-

Notes for Leaders

haps they did not graduate from high school, or recently lost a job, or failed an exam, or did poorly in a performance evaluation at work. Help them remember that Jesus knows our weaknesses (our last study) but still finds things to celebrate in our lives. We have life, relationships, friends and the love of people close to us. We are surrounded by the beauty of creation. We have Jesus and his power. Don't ignore their pain, but all members need to be reminded of things we can celebrate.

Encountering Jesus (15 minutes). Jesus is taking a bit of a risk. After all, we read in other places that there were demons the disciples could not cast out. He entrusts his ministry to people with little training and who have not yet proved themselves. But how else will they learn? He sends them out and prays for their success. He is unthreatened by their success because he sees the bigger picture of God's kingdom. What does that tell you about Jesus' character?

We can also assume that Jesus longs for his followers to experience success so that he can build them up and encourage them. He has promised that they will have power (Mark 3:13-19), and now he is letting them exercise it.

The work Jesus gives these followers, proclaiming the good news of the kingdom, is straight from God—a message proclaimed by Jesus himself. It is a message of life and hope, truth and forgiveness. People who reject the message reject the messenger. These seventy-two are acting in his name as his representatives, so rejecting the message is like rejecting Jesus. Those who reject the message are hardhearted, in denial or ignorant of their sin; they are unwilling to humbly ask more questions and consider the teachings of Jesus.

At first the disciples may have been afraid, especially as "sheep among wolves." The mission looks difficult, but they have seen Jesus model the way to carry it out, and they are not going out alone. So they probably obey with a sense of enthusiasm on one hand and fear on the other. But after great success, imagine how they feel! Verse 17 is a statement of joy and pride. And Jesus joins in the celebration.

Joining the Conversation (20 minutes). As they launch out in faith and in obedience to Christ (the first step), they receive power. Jesus sends them two by two for several reasons. It was customary in those days, for protection and companionship, and it provided the "double witness" required by Jewish law (see Deuteronomy 19:15). Every accusation was to be confirmed by two or three witnesses, so if there was something to report or to defend, it was good to have a partner. The main thing here is partnership and power in numbers. One can be praying silently while the other is sharing the good news of the kingdom.

The kingdom of God is full of paradoxes: the last shall be first, you're strong when you're weak, to gain your life you have to lose it. While the disciples appear to be successful in this mission, outward achievement is not the most important measure of our ministry success. Casting out demons is exciting, but it is not the litmus test for a saving relationship with Christ. Look at Matthew 7:21-23. There we see that casting out demons and performing miracles doesn't guarantee salvation or relationship with Jesus.

The most important thing, the thing that matters in the end, is that we act not for our own glory but to do God's will. And throughout the Bible (see especially John 15), the will of God is that we love him and love other people. Is our motive love? That matters more than our actions.

Jesus celebrates the success of the seventy-two but reminds them that there is reason for even greater joy—they know him and have an eternal destiny in heaven. So while he celebrates what they have done, it's not nearly as important as whose they are—his friends. The relationship with him is what is primary. Our success stems from obedience in the context of that relationship, not just from our own efforts.

Connecting Our Stories (20 minutes). Failure is not final. We can learn from failure and trust that Jesus can redeem any failed situation or decision. The Bible is full of stories of sinners and failures. Adam and Eve's disobedience, Jacob's lying, Moses' reluctance, King David's murder and adultery, Rahab's prostitution, Jonah's rebellion, Peter's denial, a Samaritan woman's promiscuousness, Saul's (Paul's) persecution of Christians are but a few examples. This may give some insight into how amazing Jesus is. He can forgive and look past such blunders and celebrate what he is doing in us.

Jesus refers to his disciples as "children" because they are not learned, wise and self-promoting "fathers" as some Pharisees believe themselves to be. They are just babes in Christ, willing to step out and believe. No analysis, no critique, just simple obedience and a sense of wonder that they succeed—like a kid who scores her first soccer goal: "I did it! I did it!"

Finding Our Way (10 minutes). As the group thinks about ways to serve

Notes for Leaders

and lead, remind them that Jesus did not send any of the disciples out alone—they all went two by two, so that they would have support, encouragement and accountability. Encourage your group members to think about ways that they can work together to do God's will and to test their motives so that they are not doing "religious" activities just to boost their reputation. While your group members probably won't go out on a missionary journey to preach and cast out demons, encourage them to think about their daily lives as a mission to share God's love and truth. Perhaps there are ways to hook up with your church to serve the poor and others in need.

Praying Together (about 10 minutes). Encourage the group to "rejoice that your names are written in heaven." If there are members who have not accepted Christ as their personal Savior and forgiver, this may be an opportunity to talk about what that means. Be open to the opportunity (but don't force the issue!) to tell someone how to surrender their life to Christ.

Also remember that regardless of how others view us, Jesus celebrates our successes.

Also available from InterVarsity Press and Willow Creek Resources

BIBLE 101. *Where truth meets life.*
Bill Donahue, series editor

The Bible 101 series is designed for those who want to know how to study God's Word, understand it clearly and apply it to their lives in a way that produces personal transformation. Geared especially for groups, the series can also profitably be used for individual study. Each guide has five sessions that overview essential information and teach new study skills. The sixth session brings the skills together in a way that relates them to daily life.

FOUNDATIONS: *How We Got Our Bible*
Bill Donahue

TIMES & PLACES: *Picturing the Events of the Bible*
Michael Redding

COVER TO COVER: *Getting the Bible's Big Picture*
Gerry Mathisen

STUDY METHODS: *Experiencing the Power of God's Word*
Kathy Dice

INTERPRETATION: *Discovering the Bible for Yourself*
Judson Poling

PARABLES & PROPHECY: *Unlocking the Bible's Mysteries*
Bill Donahue

GREAT THEMES: *Understanding the Bible's Core Doctrines*
Michael Redding

PERSONAL DEVOTION: *Taking God's Word to Heart*
Kathy Dice